Overview of the New Testament

PARTICIPANT'S BOOK

Stephen J. Binz

Little Rock Scripture Study

THE LITURGICAL PRESS
St. John's Abbey
Collegeville, Minnesota 56321

DIOCESE OF LITTLE ROCK
2415 North Tyler Street
P.O. Box 7239, Forest Park Station
LITTLE ROCK, ARKANSAS 72217

Telephone
Area Code 501
664-0340

Office of the Bishop

Dear Friends in Christ,

I commend you for your commitment to the study of sacred Scripture. Our tradition has always insisted that the Bible is foundational for our relationship with God. It must be at the heart of our teaching, worship, and practice as followers of Christ.

St. Jerome proclaimed, "Ignorance of Scripture is ignorance of Christ." Studying the Scriptures enables us to know Christ, to share our faith with our neighbors, and to pass on that faith to the next generation.

The Bible is the Word of God in human words. So the more we can understand its history, its language, and its literary forms, the more we can understand the revelation of God to us. For we know in faith that the same Holy Spirit who inspired the Scriptures also works within us as we read and study the Bible as God's Church.

This video-based course will help you understand the Bible better. It will show you how to read the Bible, not only for information, but to experience the living presence of God in every aspect of your life.

Your friend,

✝ Andrew J. McDonald
Bishop of Little Rock

CONTENTS

Introduction

Overview of the New Testament is a broad survey of the twenty-seven books of the New Testament. It will provide you with a general introduction to the content and themes of each writing and an understanding of the historical background of each book. As you study the meaning of each writing for the early Church, you will be encouraged to connect these writings to your own life today.

For experienced Bible users, this study will connect those books of the Bible already studied with the whole of salvation history. For Bible beginners, it will be like looking at a map before setting out on the journey of Bible study. For all participants, this overview will whet your appetite and provide a context for ongoing reading and study of the Scriptures.

The program takes an experiential approach to learning consisting of prayer, home study, group discussion, and video lectures. It is designed to be used with a group of people who will provide encouragement, support, and shared insight for one another. Through listening, reflecting, praying, and conversing, participants will come to a fuller understanding of the living Word of God.

Elements of the Program

PRAYER

Prayer is an integral part of a faith-filled study of the Bible. Each weekly session begins with a prayer service. The service will help you open your mind and heart to God's Word and reflect on some aspect of the Bible to be studied in the lesson to follow.

You are also encouraged to pray privately during the week before and after you read the Bible. Reading Scripture is an opportunity to listen to God who loves you. Pray that the same Holy Spirit who inspired the Scriptures will guide you to corrrectly understand what you read and empower you to make what you read a part of your life.

PERSONAL STUDY

Between each session you are encouraged to study the Bible at home. The only resources you need are a modern translation of the Bible and this Participant's Book. You will find questions in this book to guide your home study. Space is provided for writing your responses to each question.

The home study continues to explore the information given in the weekly lectures. Some questions will deepen your understanding of what you learned; others will anticipate the material to be covered in the next lecture. Many questions will synthesize the elements learned from the program and encourage a personal application of the Scriptures to your contemporary life.

Daily prayer, reading, and study of the Bible is a good habit to establish. Writing your responses will help you organize and clarify your thoughts.

GROUP DISCUSSION

Your written responses to the questions for home study will form the basis of the weekly group discussion. The discussion allows you to grow in your understanding as you share insights with others in the group. You will begin to build a supportive community that encourages one another to continue daily reflection on the Scriptures.

TAPED LECTURES

The informational content of this program will be provided through a series of lectures on videotape. These lectures are outlined in this book so that you will be able to follow along and add your own notes if you wish.

The first four lectures will survey the writings of Matthew, Mark, Luke, and John. They will help you understand how the New Testament fulfills the Old Testament and how the Gospels developed. The lectures will describe the unique teachings and characteristics of each writer and will survey the Synoptic Gospels, the Acts of the Apostles, and the Gospel and letters of John.

Lectures five and six give an overview of the writings of Paul. His life and message will be discussed and a description of each of the

Pauline letters will be offered. The questions and challenges of the communities to which Paul wrote will be considered in comparison to the experiences of the Church today.

The seventh lecture will describe the theology contained in the Letter to the Hebrews and the Catholic Letters. The ancient letters of James, Peter, and Jude offer guidance for the challenges of faith which we encounter today. The eighth lecture will introduce the Book of Revelation and describe the message of hope it offers for people in every age.

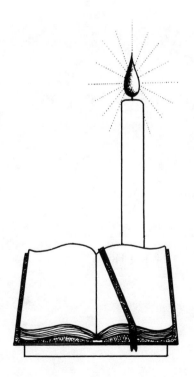

SCHEDULE FOR <u>FOUR</u> WEEKLY SESSIONS

Week 1   Date: _____

> *Prayer Service:* "Moses, Elijah, and Jesus—The Law and the Prophets Fulfilled"   p. 11
> *Lecture 1*   p. 28
> *Discussion Questions 1–6*   p. 68
> *Lecture 2*   p. 32
> *Closing*
>
> *Personal Study*—Complete Questions 7–12   p. 72

Week 2   Date: _____

> *Prayer Service:* "Mother of Jesus and Model of Faith"   p. 15
> *Lecture 3*   p. 36
> *Discussion Questions 7–12*   p. 72
> *Lecture 4*   p. 41
> *Closing*
>
> *Personal Study*—Complete Questions 13–18   p. 78

Week 3   Date: _____

> *Prayer Service:* "Chosen to Evangelize the Nations"   p. 19
> *Lecture 5*   p. 47
> *Discussion Questions 13–18*   p. 78
> *Lecture 6*   p. 54
> *Closing*
>
> *Personal Study*—Complete Questions 19–24   p. 84

Week 4   Date: _____

> *Prayer Service:* "Baptismal Birth to a Living Hope"   p. 23
> *Lecture 7*   p. 59
> *Discussion Questions 19–24*   p. 84
> *Lecture 8*   p. 64
> *Closing*

SCHEDULE FOR <u>EIGHT</u> WEEKLY SESSIONS

Week 1   Date: _____

Prayer Service: "Moses, Elijah, and Jesus—The Law and the Prophets Fulfilled"   p. 11
Lecture 1   p. 28
Discussion Questions 1–3   p. 68
Closing

Personal Study—Complete Questions 4–6   p. 70

Week 2   Date: _____

Prayer Service: "The Kingdom of God Is at Hand"   p. 13
Lecture 2   p. 32
Discussion Questions 4–6   p. 70
Closing

Personal Study—Complete Questions 7–9   p. 72

Week 3   Date: _____

Prayer Service: "Mother of Jesus and Model of Faith"   p. 15
Lecture 3   p. 36
Discussion Questions 7–9   p. 72
Closing

Personal Study—Complete Questions 10–12   p. 74

Week 4   Date: _____

Prayer Service: "Receive the Holy Spirit"   p. 17
Lecture 4   p. 41
Discussion Questions 10–12   p. 74
Closing

Personal Study—Complete Questions 13–15   p. 78

Week 5   Date: _____

Prayer Service: "Chosen to Evangelize the Nations" p. 19
Lecture 5 p. 47
Discussion Questions 13–15 p. 78
Closing

Personal Study—Complete Questions 16–18 p. 80

Week 6   Date: _____

Prayer Service: "Serving the Lord with Joyful Humility" p. 21
Lecture 6 p. 54
Discussion Questions 16–18 p. 80
Closing

Personal Study—Complete Questions 19–21 p. 84

Week 7   Date: _____

Prayer Service: "Baptismal Birth to a Living Hope" p. 23
Lecture 7 p. 59
Discussion Questions 19–21 p. 84
Closing

Personal Study—Complete Questions 22–24 p. 86

Week 8   Date: _____

Prayer Service: "Christ—The Alpha and the Omega, the Beginning
    and the End" p. 26
Lecture 8 p. 64
Discussion Questions 22–24 p. 86
Closing

Moses, Elijah, and Jesus—
The Law and the Prophets Fulfilled

Leader: God of our ancestors, you revealed yourself to Moses and Elijah on the mountain, and you revealed the glory of your Son to his disciples on the Mount of Transfiguration. As Jesus stood before Peter, James, and John, you commanded them to "listen to him." Help us to listen to the words of the Gospel so that we may know Jesus, your Son, and our Lord.

Reader: *Matthew 17:1-8*

Response: *Psalm 68:9, 17-19, 35-36*

Left: The earth quaked, the heavens shook,
before God, the One of Sinai,
before God, the God of Israel.

Right: You rugged mountains, why look with envy
at the mountain where God has chosen to dwell,
where the LORD resides forever?

Left: God's chariots were myriad, thousands upon thousands;
from Sinai the Lord entered the holy place.

Right: You went up to its lofty height;
you took captives, received slaves as tribute.
No rebels can live in the presence of God.

Left: Confess the power of God,
whose majesty protects Israel,
whose power is in the sky.

Right: Awesome is God in his holy place,
the God of Israel,
who gives power and strength to his people.

Leader: "After Moses had gone up, a cloud covered the mountain. The glory of the LORD settled upon Mount Sinai. The cloud covered it for six days, and on the seventh day he called to Moses from the midst of the cloud. To the Israelites the glory of the LORD was seen as a consuming fire on the mountaintop." *(Exod 24:15-17)*

All: "If you wish, I will make three tents here, one for you, one for Moses, and one for Elijah."

Leader: "Then the LORD said, 'Go outside and stand on the mountain before the LORD; the LORD will be passing by.' A strong and heavy wind was rending the mountains and crushing rocks before the LORD—but the LORD was not in the wind. After the wind there was an earthquake—but the LORD was not in the earthquake. After the earthquake there was fire—but the LORD was not in the fire. After the fire there was a tiny whispering sound. When he heard this, Elijah hid his face in his cloak and went and stood at the entrance of the cave." *(1 Kgs 19:11-13)*

All: "If you wish, I will make three tents here, one for you, one for Moses, and one for Elijah."

Leader: "And behold, Moses and Elijah appeared to them, conversing with him. Then Peter said to Jesus in reply, 'Lord, it is good that we are here.'"

All: "If you wish, I will make three tents here, one for you, one for Moses, and one for Elijah."

Leader: "While he was still speaking, behold, a bright cloud cast a shadow over them, then from the cloud came a voice that said, 'This is my beloved Son, with whom I am well pleased; listen to him.'"

The Kingdom of God Is at Hand

Leader: God of our Lord Jesus Christ, your Kingdom is at hand. Through Jesus, your Kingdom has come among us, yet we await its perfection in glory. Help us to pray and work for the fruitful growth of the Kingdom among us as we await the harvest to come.

Reader: Let us listen to the words of the Gospel as we hear Jesus teaching about the Kingdom by way of parables.

Mark 4:26-29, 33

Response: *Psalm 65:10-14*

Leader: You visit the earth and water it,
　　make it abundantly fertile.
God's stream is filled with water;
　　with it you supply the world with grain.

All: The seed that falls on good ground will yield a fruitful harvest.

Leader: Thus do you prepare the earth:
　　you drench plowed furrows,
　　and level their ridges.
With showers you keep the ground soft,
　　blessing its young sprouts.

All: The seed that falls on good ground will yield a fruitful harvest.

Leader: You adorn the year with your bounty;
　　your paths drip with fruitful rain.
The untilled meadows also drip;
　　the hills are robed with joy.

All: The seed that falls on good ground will yield a fruitful harvest.

Leader: The pastures are clothed with flocks,
the valleys blanketed with grain;
they cheer and sing for joy.

All: The seed that falls on good ground will yield a fruitful harvest.

Leader: Let us pray for the coming of God's Kingdom as Jesus taught us.

All: Our Father . . .

Mother of Jesus and Model of Faith

Leader: Mary is honored in Luke's Gospel because she is both the Mother of Jesus and model of faith for us. From the Annunciation to Pentecost, Mary is shown to be the ideal disciple. She hears God's Word, she believes it, and she surrenders her life to it.

Reader: Let us listen to the words of Luke's Gospel as he described the visitation of Mary to Elizabeth.

Luke 1:41-45

Response: *Luke 1:46-55*

Left: And Mary said:
"My soul proclaims the greatness of the Lord;
   my spirit rejoices in God my savior.
For he has looked upon his handmaid's lowliness;
   behold, from now on will all ages call me blessed.

Right: The Mighty One has done great things for me,
   and holy is his name.
His mercy is from age to age
   to those who fear him.

Left: He has shown might with his arm,
   dispersed the arrogant of mind and heart.
He has thrown down the rulers from their thrones
   but lifted up the lowly.

Right: The hungry he has filled with good things;
   the rich he has sent away empty.
He has helped Israel his servant,
   remembering his mercy,
according to his promise to our fathers,
   to Abraham and his descendants forever."

Leader: Mary said, "Behold, I am the handmaid of the Lord. May it be done to me according to your word." *(1:38)*

All: Hail Mary . . .

Leader: Jesus said: "My mother and my brothers are those who hear the word of God and act on it." *(8:21)*

All: Hail Mary . . .

Leader: When they entered the city they went to the upper room where they were staying, Peter and John and James and Andrew, Philip and Thomas, Bartholomew and Matthew, James son of Alphaeus, Simon the Zealot, and Judas son of James. All these devoted themselves with one accord to prayer, together with some women, and Mary the mother of Jesus, and his brothers. *(Acts 1:13-14)*

All: Hail Mary . . .

Receive the Holy Spirit

Leader: Jesus said: "The hour is coming, and is now here, when true worshipers will worship the Father in Spirit and truth; and indeed the Father seeks such people to worship him. God is Spirit, and those who worship him must worship in Spirit and truth." *(John 4:23-24)* Jesus teaches that it is the Holy Spirit which enables disciples to know God and to worship God. Let us listen to the words of Jesus from the Gospel according to John.

Reader 1: Thomas said to him, "Master, we do not know where you are going; how can we know the way?" Jesus said to him, "I am the way and the truth and the life. No one comes to the Father except through me. If you know me, then you will also know my Father." *(John 14:5-7)*

All: Come Holy Spirit, fill the hearts of your faithful and kindle in them the fire of your love.

Reader 2: "And I will ask the Father, and he will give you another Advocate to be with you always, the Spirit of truth, which the world cannot accept, because it neither sees nor knows it. But you know it, because it remains with you, and will be in you." *(John 14:16-17)*

All: Come Holy Spirit, fill the hearts of your faithful and kindle in them the fire of your love.

Reader 3: "I have told you this while I am with you. The Advocate, the holy Spirit that the Father will send in my name—he will teach you everything and remind you of all that [I] told you." *(John 14:25-26)*

All: Come Holy Spirit, fill the hearts of your faithful and kindle in them the fire of your love.

Reader 4: "I have much more to tell you, but you cannot bear it now. But when he comes, the Spirit of truth, he will guide you to all truth." *(John 16:12-13)*

All: Come Holy Spirit, fill the hearts of your faithful and kindle in them the fire of your love. Send forth your Spirit and they will be recreated, and you shall renew the face of the earth.

Leader: When the disciples of Jesus were hiding in fear behind locked doors, the risen Jesus stood in their midst and said to them, "Peace be with you. As the Father has sent me, so I send you." And when he had said this, he breathed on them and said to them, "Receive the holy Spirit." *(John 20:19-22)*

All: Come Holy Spirit, guide us so that we may know Jesus Christ more fully. Teach us and remind us of everything that he told us, so that we may be directed to all truth. Motivate our hearts so that we can act on his word, to be sent into the world to live the truth of the Gospel.

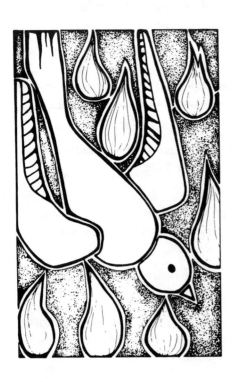

Chosen to Evangelize the Nations

Leader: God of all nations and peoples, you chose Paul to bring the message of salvation beyond the people of Israel. Because you called him and sent him out, Paul became the Church's great missionary to the Gentiles. Enliven us with the commission to evangelize the society in which we live, so that the Gospel of Jesus may continue to be proclaimed to the people of our time.

Reader 1: Let us listen to the account of Paul's conversion from the Acts of the Apostles.

Acts 9:1-20

Response: *Psalm 117*

All: "Go into the whole world and proclaim the gospel to every creature." *(Mark 16:15)*

Leader: Praise the LORD, all you nations!
   Give glory, all you peoples!

All: "Go into the whole world and proclaim the gospel to every creature."

Leader: The LORD's love for us is strong;
   the LORD is faithful forever.

All: "Go into the whole world and proclaim the gospel to every creature."

Leader 2: Let us listen to the words of the encyclical, "Evangelization in the Modern World."

"We wish to affirm once more that the essential mission of the Church is to evangelize all people. It is a task and mission which the great and fundamental changes of contemporary society make all the more urgent. Evangelization is the special grace and vocation of the Church. It is her essential function . . . . For the Christian community can never be confined within itself, because its intimate life, this is its zeal for prayer, its hearing of the word and teaching of the apostles, its exercise of fraternal charity, the breaking of the bread, cannot achieve its full force and value unless it becomes a witness and evokes admiration and conversion of souls. It must preach the gospel and announce the good news. In this way the mission of evangelization is undertaken by the whole Church and the work of each individual redounds to the good of all." (*Evangelii Nuntiandi,* 14–15)

Leader: May God who has given us faith and enriched us through the Scriptures, the sacraments, and the life of Christ's Church, give us a burning desire to share the good things we have received.

All: Glory be to the Father, and to the Son, and to the Holy Spirit, as it was in the beginning, is now, and ever shall be, world without end. Amen.

Serving the Lord with Joyful Humility

Leader: Grace to you and peace from God our Father and the Lord Jesus Christ. *(Phil 1:2)*

All: And also with you.

Reader: Let us listen to the words of Paul's letter to the Philippians as he expresses gratitude for the privilege of serving the Gospel.

Philippians 1:3-11

Response: *Philippians 2:5-11*

All: Have among yourselves the same attitude that is also yours in Christ Jesus,
Who, though he was in the form of God,
   did not regard equality with God something to be
     grasped.
   Rather, he emptied himself,
   taking the form of a slave,
   coming in human likeness;
   and found human in appearance,
   he humbled himself,
   becoming obedient to death,
     even death on a cross.
Because of this, God greatly exalted him
   and bestowed upon him the name
   that is above every name,
   that at the name of Jesus
   every knee should bend,
   of those in heaven and on earth and under the earth,
   and every tongue confess that
   Jesus Christ is Lord,
   to the glory of God the Father.

Leader: Let us now voice the prayers that arise from our hearts. Please respond: "Graciously hear us, O God."

(All are invited to express their prayers of petition aloud.)

Leader: Have no anxiety at all, but in everything, by prayer and petition, with thanksgiving, make your requests known to God. Then the peace of God that surpasses all understanding will guard your hearts and minds in Christ Jesus. *(Phil 4:6-7)*

Baptismal Birth to a Living Hope

Leader: God, who has given us life and a new birth in Jesus Christ, you have chosen us to be a priestly people. Through the grace of our Baptism, help us to share in the mission of your Church, offering spiritual sacrifices and witnessing to the hope you have given us.

Reader 1: Let us listen to the words of the First Letter of Peter as he praises God who gives us new life and hope through our Baptism.

1 Peter 1:3-9

Response: *Psalm 42:2-3; 43:3-4*

Leader: As the deer longs for streams of water,
    so my soul longs for you, O God.
My being thirsts for God, the living God.
    When can I go and see the face of God?

All: My soul is thirsting for the living God.

Leader: Send your light and fidelity,
    that they may be my guide
And bring me to your holy mountain,
    to the place of your dwelling.

All: My soul is thirsting for the living God.

Leader: That I may come to the altar of God,
    to God, my joy, my delight.
Then I will praise you with the harp,
    O God, my God.

All: My soul is thirsting for the living God.

Reader 2: Let us listen to the words of the Dogmatic Constitution on the Church as it proclaims the dignity of our baptismal consecration.

Christ the Lord, high priest taken from among men (cf. *Heb 5:1-5*), made the new people "a kingdom of priests to God, his Father" *(Rev 1:6;* cf. *5:9-10).* The baptized, by regeneration and the anointing of the Holy Spirit, are consecrated to be a spiritual house and a holy priesthood, that through all the works of Christian men they may offer spiritual sacrifices and proclaim the perfection of him who has called them out of darkness into his marvelous light (cf. *1 Pet 2:4-10).* Therefore all the disciples of Christ, persevering in prayer and praising God (cf. *Acts 2:42-47),* should present themselves as a sacrifice, living, holy, and pleasing to God (cf. *Rom 12:1).* They should everywhere on earth bear witness to Christ and give an answer to everyone who asks a reason for the hope of an eternal life which is theirs. (cf. *1 Pet 3:15) (Lumen Gentium,* 10)

Leader: Praise to you, God of life, for you created water to refresh, to cleanse, and to give new life. Blessed be God.

All: Let the waters of life renew us.

Leader: Through the offering of your Son on the cross and in the blood and water flowing from his side, the Church is born. Blessed be God.

All: Let the waters of life renew us.

Leader: Through your Holy Spirit, you anointed Christ at his Baptism in the Jordan, that we might all be baptized in him. Blessed be God.

All: Let the waters of life renew us.

Leader: In the tomb of baptism we have died with Christ, and in the womb of baptism we have risen with Christ to new life. Blessed be God.

All: Let the waters of life renew us.

Leader: Through the waters of Baptism you have made us a kingdom of priests to offer spiritual sacrifices to you. Blessed be God.

All: Let the waters of life renew us.

Leader: As a baptized people we are called to witness to Christ and to the hope we have been given. Blessed be God.

All: Let the waters of life renew us.

(The leader sprinkles all with holy water or all approach the bowl of water and cross themselves.)

Leader: May the God of life renew our Baptism and enliven us for service in the name of Jesus, the Lord.

All: Amen.

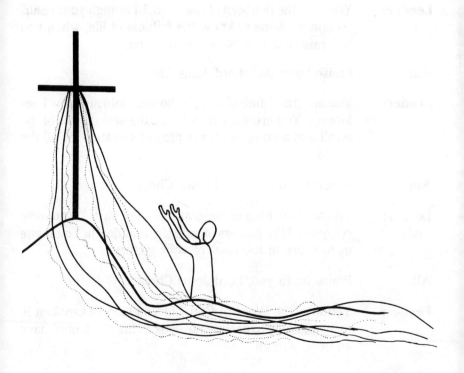

Christ—The Alpha and the Omega, the Beginning and the End

Leader: God, our Creator and our Redeemer, you call all people to salvation, to experience victory over sin and death through the passion and resurrection of Christ. Help us to look to the future with hope in your promises.

Reader: A Reading from the Book of Revelation

Revelation 19:5-10

Leader: You are "the alpha and the omega, the beginning and the end." Through you all things were made, and through you history will come to its completion.

All: Praise be to you, Lord Jesus Christ.

Leader: You are "the firstborn of the dead." Through your resurrection we hope to know the fullness of life, when you will raise our bodies to life with you.

All: Praise be to you, Lord Jesus Christ.

Leader: You are "the Lamb of God," who was slain and now lives forever. You are worthy to break the seven seals of the scroll and accomplish God's plan of salvation for all the world.

All: Praise be to you, Lord Jesus Christ.

Leader: You are "the King of kings and Lord of lords." You have conquered the powers of evil, sin, and death. You invite us to share in the feast of your victory.

All: Praise be to you, Lord Jesus Christ.

Leader: You are "the Word of God." In you God has spoken finally and fully to us. In your book of life our names have all been written.

All: Praise be to you, Lord Jesus Christ.

Leader: You are invited to approach the Bible and place your hands upon it as a sign of your desire to continue knowing Christ through the Sacred Scriptures.

(All come forward in silence.)

Leader: May the peace of our Lord Jesus Christ be with you always.

All: And also with you.

Leader: Let us offer to one another a sign of the peace of Christ.

LECTURE 1—THE GOSPELS:
THE GOOD NEWS OF JESUS CHRIST

I. Introduction—The Old anticipates the New

   A. The faith of Israel fulfilled in Christ

   "These are my words that I spoke to you while I was still with you, that everything written about me in the law of Moses and in the prophets and psalms must be fulfilled." *(Luke 24:44)*

   B. Persons, events, and institutions of the Old Testament foreshadow Christ

   "Moreover, all the prophets who spoke, from Samuel and those afterwards, also announced these days. You are the children of the prophets and of the covenant that God made with your ancestors when he said to Abraham, 'In your offspring all the families of the earth shall be blessed.'" *(Acts 3:24-25)*

   C. The Old and New Testaments are intimately united

   1. They are both centered on faith in the one God.

   2. They form one divine plan of salvation.

   3. They are connected historically through the faith of Israel.

   4. The New Testament themes and vocabulary are based on the Old.

   5. They are related by promise and fulfillment.

   6. They look to the same future.

II. Messianic Expectation

    A. The person of the Messiah

        1. Son of David

        2. Son of Man

        3. Suffering Servant

    B. The messianic Kingdom

        "This is the time of fulfillment. The kingdom of God is at hand. Repent, and believe in the gospel." *(Mark 1:15)*

III. The Gospel of Jesus Christ

    A. The "good news" of his life, death, and resurrection

    B. Four unique portraits of Jesus—The Gospels according to Matthew, Mark, Luke, and John

    C. Development of the Gospels

        1. The earthly life of Jesus—first third of the first century

2. Proclaiming and teaching the good news of Jesus—second third of the first century

3. Writing the four Gospels—final third of the first century

D. The Gospels as two-level documents

1. The historical context of Jesus

a. The regions of Galilee, Samaria, and Judea

b. The temple and the synagogue

c. The Jewish feasts of Passover, Pentecost, and Tabernacles

d. The Sabbath

2. The historical context of each evangelist

a. Greek language and thought

b. Written in different parts of the world

c. Written to distinct audiences

PALESTINE IN THE TIME OF JESUS

Miles
0 _____ 40

Kms
0 _____ 40

MEDITERRANEAN

SEA

Abila •
ABILENE

Damascus •

Sidon •

Zarephath •

PHOENICIA

LEBANON MTS.

SYRIA

▲ MT. HERMON

Tyre •

• Caesarea Philippi

GALILEE

Ptolemais •

Chorazin •   • Bethsaida
Capernaum •
                    Lake
Magadan •
Cana •   Tiberias •   Galilee
    • Nazareth
Nain •   ▲ MT.
         TABOR   • Gadara

MT. CARMEL ▲

Caesarea •

TEN TOWNS

• Salim

SAMARIA

Aenon •

Samaria •
         ▲ MT. EBAL
MT. GERIZIM ▲ • Sychar

• Gerasa

Joppa •

Arimathea? •

Ephraim •

Jordan River

PEREA

Jericho •   • Bethany

Emmaus •
Jerusalem • •   Bethany
         Qumran •

Azotus •

Ascalon •

JUDEA   • Bethlehem

Gaza •

• Hebron   Dead

Sea

IDUMEA

N A B A T E A

© United Bible Societies, 1978

LECTURE 2—THE GOSPELS: THE SYNOPTIC TRADITION

I. Similar and Different—History and Interpretation

   A. Synoptic—Matthew, Mark, and Luke

   B. "Synopsis of the Gospels"

II. Three principles of composition

   A. Selectivity

   B. Arrangement

   C. Adaptation

III. The Gospel of Matthew

   A. Jesus Christ fulfills the law and the prophets

     "Jesus Christ, the son of David, the son of Abraham." *(Matt 1:1)*

     "Go, therefore, and make disciples of all nations." *(Matt 28:19)*

B. Five-book structure

Prologue—the infancy narrative (1–2)

1. The beginnings of Jesus' ministry (3–4)

    The Sermon on the Mount (5–7)

2. Expanding ministry and miracles (8–9)

    Missionary discourse (10)

3. Controversy and opposition (11–12)

    Parable discourse (13)

4. Formation of disciples (14–17)

    Discourse on church order and community (18)

5. Ministry in Judea (19–22)

    Eschatological discourse (23–25)

Conclusion—the passion and resurrection narrative (26–28)

C. Jesus as the great teacher

1. The Sermon on the Mount

    "When he saw the crowds, he went up the mountain, and after he had sat down, his disciples came to him. He began to teach them. . . ." *(Matt 5:1-2)*

2. The parables of the Kingdom

"This is why I speak to them in parables, because 'they look but do not see and hear but do not listen or understand. . . .'" *(Matt 13:13)*

D. The Gospel of the Church

1. Opposition to the Pharisees

2. Community of all the nations, Jews and Gentiles

3. God-with-us

"Behold, I am with you always, until the end of the age." *(Matt 28:20)*

IV. The Gospel of Mark

A. Sources of the Gospel

1. Oral and written tradition

2. Mark's insights on the meaning of Jesus' life

B. Fundamental questions of Mark's Gospel

1. Who is Jesus?—understanding Jesus

2. How do I follow him?—understanding discipleship

C. Opening verse offers a preview and structure

The beginning of the gospel of Jesus Christ [the Son of God].
(Mark 1:1)

"Who do you say that I am?" *(Mark 8:29)*

1. Jesus as the Christ climaxes the first half

"You are the Messiah." *(Mark 8:29)* / Christ / Anointed
One—Peter proclaims an incomplete understanding of Jesus'
identity.

2. Jesus as the Son of God climaxes the second half

"Truly this man was the son of God!" *(Mark 15:39)*—At the
cross the full identity of Jesus is understood.

D. Lessons in discipleship

1. Passion predictions of Jesus met by misunderstanding and
resistance

2. Healing from blindness, sign of healing disciples of spiritual
blindness

3. Failure of disciples at the passion

4. Minor characters as examples of discipleship

LECTURE 3—THE LUKAN WRITINGS:
THE GOSPEL AND ACTS

I. Stages of Salvation History—Jesus as Savior of All Nations

    A. Period of Israel—creation to John the Baptist

       "The law and the prophets lasted until John; but from then on the kingdom of God is proclaimed." *(Luke 16:16)*

    B. Period of Jesus—public ministry of Jesus to ascension

       "The Spirit of the Lord is upon me,
         because he has anointed me to bring glad tidings to the poor.
       He has sent me to proclaim liberty to captives
         and recovery of sight to the blind,
           to let the oppressed go free,
       and to proclaim a year acceptable to the Lord."

       "Rolling up the scroll, he handed it back to the attendant and sat down, and the eyes of all in the synagogue looked intently at him. He said to them, 'Today this scripture passage is fulfilled in your hearing.'" *(Luke 4:18-21)*

    C. Period of the Church—ascension to the end of history

II. The Journey of Jesus and of the Early Church

    A. Structure of the Gospel

Prologue—the infancy narrative (1–2) and preparation for ministry (3:1–4:13)

1. Ministry in Galilee (4:14–9:50)

2. Journey to Jerusalem (9:51–19:27)

3. Teaching in Jerusalem (19:28–21:38) and Passion, Death, and Resurrection (22–24)

B. Structure of Acts of the Apostles

1. In Jerusalem (1–7)

2. Outward into Judea and Samaria (8–9)

3. Into the Gentile world of Syria, Asia Minor, and Europe (10–28)

"You will receive power when the holy Spirit comes upon you, and you will be my witnesses in Jerusalem, throughout Judea and Samaria, and to the ends of the earth." *(Acts 1:8)*

C. Jerusalem and Rome—goals of the journey

". . . repentance, for the forgiveness of sins, would be preached in his name to all the nations, beginning from Jerusalem." *(Luke 24:47)*

"And thus we came to Rome." *(Acts 28:14)*

D. We continue the journey, following "the Way."

III. The Acts of the Apostles

    A. Theological history

    B. Parallel focus on Peter and Paul

        1. The prominence of Peter (1–12)

        2. The shift of attention to Paul (13–28)

    C. The life of Jesus continues in the life of the Church

IV. Characteristics of Luke's writings

    A. The role of the Holy Spirit

        1. Forms the transitions from Israel, to Jesus, to the Church

        2. The Acts of the Holy Spirit

    B. Prayer

        1. People of prayer—the Songs of Mary, Zechariah, Simeon

        2. The prayer of Jesus

3. Jesus taught his disciples to pray

C. Merciful forgiveness

"Be merciful, just as [also] your Father is merciful." *(Luke 6:36)*

"Father, forgive them, they know not what they do." *(Luke 23:34)*

"Today you will be with me in Paradise." *(Luke 23:43)*

D. Universality of salvation

1. Salvation for Jews and Gentiles

"Now, Master, you may let your servant go in peace, according to your word, for my eyes have seen your salvation, which you prepared in sight of all the peoples, a light for revelation to the Gentiles, and glory for your people Israel." *(Luke 2:29-32)*

"People will come from the east and the west and from the north and the south and will recline at table in the kingdom of God." *(Luke 13:29)*

"Let it be known to you that this salvation of God has been sent to the Gentiles." *(Acts 28:28)*

2. Concern for the rejected

a. Parable of the Good Samaritan

b. Parable of the Rich Man and Lazarus

c. Parable of the Pharisee and the Tax Collector

    d. Parables of the Lost Sheep, the Lost Coin, and the Lost Son

"For the Son of Man has come to seek and to save what was lost." *(Luke 19:10)*

3. Attention to women

LECTURE 4—THE JOHANNINE WRITINGS: THE GOSPEL AND LETTERS

I. A Unique Gospel Portrait

    A. A partial view of Jesus

       "There are also many other things that Jesus did, but if these were to be described individually, I do not think the whole world would contain the books that would be written." *(John 21:25)*

    B. Different from the Synoptic Gospels

II. Development of the Gospel

    A. John and his community

    B. The "beloved disciple"

       "One of his disciples, the one whom Jesus loved, was reclining at Jesus' side." *(John 13:23)*

       "When Jesus saw his mother and the disciple there whom he loved, he said to his mother, 'Woman, behold, your son.'" *(John 19:26)*

       "An eyewitness has testified, and his testimony is true; he knows that he is speaking the truth, so that you also may [come to] believe." *(John 19:35)*

"So she ran and went to Simon Peter and to the other disciple whom Jesus loved, and told them, 'They have taken the Lord from the tomb, and we don't know where they put him.'" *(John 20:2)*

"It is this disciple who testifies to these things and has written them, and we know that his testimony is true." *(John 21:24)*

1. John, son of Zebedee

2. Model of discipleship

III. The "Signs" of the Gospel

A. The seven signs

  1. Changing water into wine at Cana

  2. Healing the royal official's son

  3. Healing the paralyzed man

  4. Feeding the five thousand

  5. Walking on the water

  6. Healing the blind man

  7. Raising Lazarus from the dead

B. Signs point to the truth of who Jesus is

C. The Exodus background for the signs of Jesus—passover lamb, the bronze serpent, the manna, the water from the rock, crossing the sea, the authority of Moses

"How long will they refuse to believe in me, despite all the signs I have performed among them?" *(Num 14:11)*

"Although he had performed so many signs in their presence they did not believe in him." *(John 12:37)*

D. Gospel written to lead us to faith

"Now Jesus did many other signs in the presence of [his] disciples that are not written in this book. But these are written that you may [come to] believe that Jesus is the Messiah, the Son of God, and that through this belief you may have life in his name." *(John 20:30-31)*

IV. The Dual Nature of Jesus—Human and Divine

A. True humanity in a physical world

B. "I AM"—God's self-revelation

"When you lift up the Son of Man, then you will realize that I AM." *(John 8:28)*

"Amen, amen, I say to you, before Abraham came to be, I AM." *(John 8:58)*

"From now on I am telling you before it happens, so that when it happens you may believe that I AM." *(John 13:19)*

C. The identity of Jesus in relationship to us

1. I am the bread of life. *(John 6:35)*

2. I am the light of the world. *(John 8:12)*

3. I am the gate for the sheep. *(John 10:7)*

4. I am the good shepherd. *(John 10:11)*

5. I am the resurrection and the life. *(John 11:25)*

6. I am the way and the truth and the life. *(John 14:6)*

7. I am the true vine. *(John 15:1)*

D. The eternal Word—The Gospel prologue

"In the beginning was the Word,
  and the Word was with God,
  and the Word was God.
He was in the beginning with God.
All things came to be through him,
  and without him nothing came to be.
What came to be through him was life,
  and this life was the light of the human race;
the light shines in the darkness,
  and the darkness has not overcome it." *(John 1:1-5)*

"And the Word became flesh
  and made his dwelling among us,

and we saw his glory,
the glory as of the Father's only Son,
full of grace and truth." *(John 1:14)*

V. The Three Letters of John

A. The challenge of balanced spirituality

B. The incarnate Word

"What was from the beginning,
what we have heard,
what we have seen with our eyes,
what we looked upon
and touched with our hands
concerns the Word of life—
for the life was made visible;
we have seen it and testify to it
and proclaim to you the eternal life
that was with the Father and was made visible to us—
what we have seen and heard
we proclaim now to you,
so that you too may have fellowship with us;
for our fellowship is with the Father
and with his Son, Jesus Christ." *(1 John 1:1-3)*

C. Major themes

1. Light

"If we walk in the light as he is in the light, then we have
fellowship with one another." *(1 John 1:7)*

2. Life

"This is the promise that he made us: eternal life." *(1 John 2:25)*

3. Love

"God is love, and whoever remains in love remains in God and God in him." *(1 John 4:16)*

LECTURE 5—THE PAULINE WRITINGS: THE GREAT LETTERS

I. Paul—Apostle and Writer

  A. Missionary correspondence to the churches

  B. Paul's experience of conversion and revelation

  C. The circumstances of Paul's life

    1. The Jewish world

      a. Diaspora Judaism

      b. Rabbi Gamaliel

      c. Judaism of the Pharisees

      d. Love for the Torah

      e. Covenant with Israel

        "I ask, then, has God rejected his people? Of course not!
        . . . For the gifts and the call of God are irrevocable."
        (Rom 11:1, 29)

    2. The Greek world

      a. Use of the Septuagint

      b. Hellenistic culture

      c. Need for unity amidst diversity

"Here there is not Greek and Jew, circumcision and un-circumcision, barbarian, Scythian, slave, free; but Christ is all and in all." *(Col 3:11)*

3. The Roman world

    a. Commerce and travel within the empire

    b. Roman citizenship

"Circumcised on the eighth day, of the race of Israel, of the tribe of Benjamin, a Hebrew of Hebrew parentage, in observance of the law a Pharisee, in zeal I persecuted the church, in righteousness based on the law I was blameless. [But] whatever gains I had, these I have come to consider a loss because of Christ. More than that, I even consider everything as a loss because of the supreme good of knowing Christ Jesus my Lord." *(Phil 3:5-8)*

II. The Letters of Paul

A. Style

B. Sources for his content

    1. Reflection on the Hebrew Scriptures

    2. Contemplating his experience of Christ

    3. Tradition handed down from the apostles

    4. Insights from missionary and pastoral experience

C. Order

D. Traditional groupings

1. Great Letters: Galatians and Romans, 1 and 2 Corinthians

2. Eschatological Letters: 1 and 2 Thessalonians

3. Captivity Letters: Philippians, Philemon, Colossians, and Ephesians

4. Pastoral Letters: 1 and 2 Timothy and Titus

III. The Letter to the Galatians

A. Background of controversy

B. Content of letter

1. Apostolic authority (1–2)

2. Christian freedom (3–4)

3. Practical consequences of freedom (5–6)

IV. The Letter to the Romans

A. Significance of Rome

B. Content of letter

   1. Need and significance of salvation (1–8)

   2. God's plan for the salvation of Israel (9–11)

   3. Consequences of salvation for Christian living (12–16)

C. Central teachings

   1. Domination of sin

     "All have sinned and are deprived of the glory of God." *(Rom 3:23)*

   2. The gift of grace

     "Where sin increased, grace overflowed all the more, so that, as sin reigned in death, grace also might reign through justification for eternal life through Jesus Christ our Lord." *(Rom 5:20-21)*

   3. Reconciliation through Christ

     "God proves his love for us in that while we were still sinners Christ died for us. How much more then, since we are now justified by his blood, will we be saved through him from the wrath. Indeed, if, while we were enemies, we were reconciled to God through the death of his Son, how much more, once reconciled, will we be saved by his life. Not only that, but we also boast of God through our Lord Jesus Christ, through whom we have now received reconciliation." *(Rom 5:8-11)*

   4. The faith that justifies

V. The Letters to the Corinthians

A. Pastoral responses to controversy and struggle in the community

" . . . I became your father in Christ Jesus through the gospel."
(1 Cor 4:15)

B. Content of First Corinthians

  1. Unity through the cross (1–6)

    "God chose the foolish of the world to shame the wise, and God chose the weak of the world to shame the strong, and God chose the lowly and despised of the world, those who count for nothing, to reduce to nothing those who are something, so that no human being might boast before God." *(1 Cor 1:27-29)*

  2. Responses to questions (7–16)

    marriage and celibacy, food sacrificed to pagan idols, the headcovering of women, abuse when celebrating Eucharist, the use of spiritual gifts, and the resurrection of the dead

C. Content of Second Corinthians

  "But we hold this treasure in earthen vessels, that the surpassing power may be of God and not from us. We are afflicted in every way, but not constrained; perplexed, but not driven to despair; persecuted, but not abandoned; struck down, but not destroyed; always carrying about in the body the dying of Jesus, so that the life of Jesus may also be manifested in our body." *(2 Cor 4:7-10)*

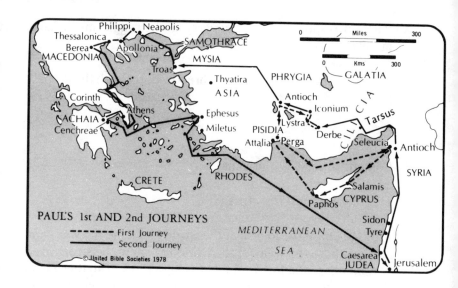

PAUL'S 1st AND 2nd JOURNEYS
- - - - First Journey
———— Second Journey
© United Bible Societies 1978

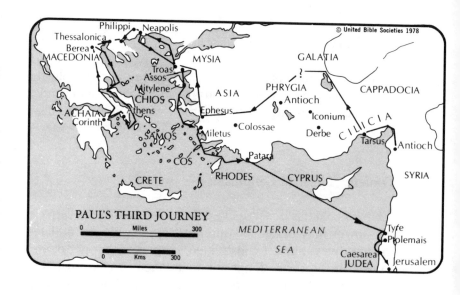

PAUL'S THIRD JOURNEY

© United Bible Societies 1978

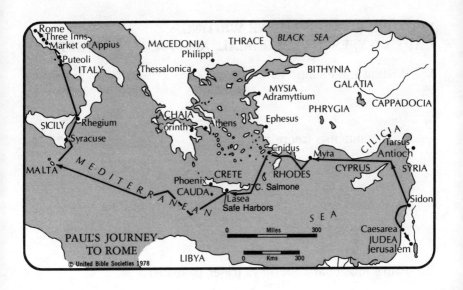

PAUL'S JOURNEY TO ROME

© United Bible Societies 1978

LECTURE 6—THE PAULINE WRITINGS: CAPTIVITY, ESCHATOLOGICAL, AND PASTORAL LETTERS

I. Writing the Pauline letters

   A. Amanuensis (secretary)

   B. Coworkers and disciples—the authority of Paul

II. Paul's Missionary Journeys (refer to maps)

III. Captivity Letters

   A. Paul's imprisonments—Corinth, Ephesus, Caesarea, and Rome

   B. Letter to the Philippians

      1. Peace and confidence while in chains

         "For to me life is Christ, and death is gain." *(Phil 1:21)*

         "Our citizenship is in heaven, and from it we also await a savior, the Lord Jesus Christ." *(Phil 3:20)*

         "So then, my beloved, obedient as you have always been, not only when I am present but all the more now when I am absent, work out your salvation with fear and trembling." *(Phil 2:12)*

2. A letter of joy

"Rejoice in the Lord always. I shall say it again: rejoice! Your kindness should be known to all. The Lord is near. Have no anxiety at all, but in everything, by prayer and petition, with thanksgiving, make your requests known to God. Then the peace of God that surpasses all understanding will guard your hearts and minds in Christ Jesus." *(Phil 4:4-7)*

C. Letter to Philemon

1. Onesimus the slave, converted and baptized

"Perhaps this is why he was away from you for a while, that you might have him back forever, no longer as a slave but more than a slave, a brother, beloved especially to me, but even more so to you, as a man and in the Lord." *(Phlm 15-16)*

2. Baptism into Christ changes relationships

D. Letter to the Colossians

1. True faith in Christ

"See to it that no one captivate you with an empty, seductive philosophy according to human tradition, according to the elemental powers of the world and not according to Christ. For in him dwells the whole fullness of the deity bodily, and you share in this fullness in him, who is the head of every principality and power." *(Col 2:8-10)*

2. Practical advice and ethical implications

"Let the word of Christ dwell in you richly, as in all wisdom you teach and admonish one another, singing psalms, hymns, and spiritual songs with gratitude in your hearts to God. And whatever you do, in word or in deed, do everything in the name of the Lord Jesus, giving thanks to God the Father through him." *(Col 3:16-17)*

E. Letter to the Ephesians

1. General and universal scope

2. The worldwide Church—the fullness of Christ

"He [God] put all things beneath his [Christ's] feet and gave him as head over all things to the church, which is his body, the fullness of the one who fills all things in every way." *(Eph 1:22-23)*

3. Since the Church is one, we must strive for unity

"I, then, a prisoner for the Lord, urge you to live in a manner worthy of the call you have received, with all humility and gentleness, with patience, bearing with one another through love, striving to preserve the unity of the spirit through the bond of peace: one body and one Spirit, as you were also called to the one hope of your call; one Lord, one faith, one baptism; one God and Father of all, who is over all and through all and in all." *(Eph 4:1-6)*

IV. Eschatological Letters—1 and 2 Thessalonians

A. Correcting misconceptions about the Lord's coming

B. Discouraging predictions; encouraging vigilance and preparation

V. Pastoral Letters

   A. Organization and direction of the churches entrusted to Timothy and Titus

   B. "Pastoral" issues in the letters

      1. Concern for sound doctrine

      2. Concern for community leadership

      3. Concern for apostolic tradition

   C. First Timothy

      1. Urges Timothy to refrain false teachers and be faithful to his task (1)

         "I entrust this charge to you, Timothy, my child, in accordance with the prophetic words once spoken about you. Through them may you fight a good fight by having faith and a good conscience. Some, by rejecting conscience, have made a shipwreck of their faith." *(1 Tim 1:18-19)*

      2. Regulations for liturgical assembly and qualifications for leadership (2–3)

         Church is "the household of God . . . the pillar and foundation of truth." *(1 Tim 3:15)*

      3. Advice for teaching and conduct (4)

         "Do not neglect the gift you have, which was conferred on you through the prophetic word with the imposition of hands of the presbyterate. Be diligent in these matters, be absorbed in them, so that your progress may be evident to everyone." *(1 Tim 4:14-15)*

4. Advice for widows, presbyters, slaves, and masters (5–6)

"O Timothy, guard what has been entrusted to you." *(1 Tim 6:20)*

D. Second Timothy

"I charge you in the presence of God and of Christ Jesus . . . proclaim the word; be persistent whether it is convenient or inconvenient; convince, reprimand, encourage through all patience and teaching. For the time will come when people will not tolerate sound doctrine but, following their own desires and insatiable curiosity, will accumulate teachers and will stop listening to the truth and will be diverted to myths. But you, be self-possessed in all circumstances; put up with hardship; perform the work of an evangelist; fulfill your ministry." *(2 Tim 4:1-5)*

E. Titus

1. Qualifications of a Christian leader

2. Guidelines for Christian behavior

"For the grace of God has appeared, saving all and training us to reject godless ways and worldly desires and to live temperately, justly, and devoutly in this age, as we await the blessed hope, the appearance of the glory of the great God and of our savior Jesus Christ." *(Titus 2:11-13)*

VI. Inspired letters for the Church of Paul and the Church of today.

LECTURE 7—THE LETTER TO THE HEBREWS AND CATHOLIC LETTERS

I. Letter to the Hebrews

A. Christians roots in the Hebrew Scriptures

"In times past, God spoke in partial and various ways to our ancestors through the prophets; in these last days, he spoke to us through a son, whom he made heir of all things." *(Heb 1:1-2)*

B. The Old gives way to the New

1. Jesus compared with Moses

"Moses was 'faithful in all his house' as a 'servant' to testify to what would be spoken, but Christ was faithful as a son placed over his house." *(Heb 3:5-6)*

2. Jesus compared to the priests in the line of Levi and to Melchizedek

"Those priests were many because they were prevented by death from remaining in office, but he, because he remains forever, has a priesthood that does not pass away. Therefore, he is always able to save those who approach God through him, since he lives forever to make intercession for them." *(Heb 7:23-25)*

3. Sacrifice of Christ compared with the Day of Atonement

"But when Christ came as high priest of the good things that have come to be, passing through the greater and more perfect tabernacle not made by hands, that is, not belonging to this creation, he entered once for all into the sanctuary, not with the blood of goats and calves but with his own blood, thus obtaining eternal redemption." *(Heb 9:11-12)*

C. Instruction and exhortation

"The word of God is living and effective, sharper than any two-edged sword." *(Heb 4:12)*

D. Summary of Israel's salvation history—a "cloud of witnesses"

E. Jesus lives and intercedes for us today

"Jesus Christ is the same yesterday, today, and forever." *(Heb 13:8)*

II. Catholic Letters

A. The Letter of James

1. Author and audience

"James, a slave of God and of the Lord Jesus Christ, to the twelve tribes in the dispersion, greetings." *(Jas 1:1)*

2. Guidance on ethical issues

"Be doers of the word and not hearers only." *(Jas 1:22)*

"See how a person is justified by works and not by faith alone. . . . For just as a body without a spirit is dead, so also faith without works is dead." *(Jas 2:24, 26)*

3. Faith in the teachings of James and Paul

B. The First Letter of Peter

1. Author and audience

"Peter, an apostle of Jesus Christ, to the chosen sojourners of the dispersion . . . ." *(1 Pet 1:1)*

2. Structure of the letter

a. Proclamation of the gospel message *(1:1–2:10)*

b. Call for responsible living *(2:11–5:14)*

3. Christian baptism and living the baptismal call

"Blessed be the God and Father of our Lord Jesus Christ, who in his great mercy gave us a new birth to a living hope through the resurrection of Jesus Christ from the dead." *(1 Pet 1:3)*

"You are 'a chosen race, a royal priesthood, a holy nation, a people of his own, so that you may announce the praises' of him who called you out of darkness into his wonderful light.
   Once you were 'no people'
      but now you are God's people;
   you 'had not received mercy'
      but now you have received mercy." *(1 Pet 2:9-10)*

4. Living in the midst of the world

"The end of all things is at hand. Therefore, be serious and sober for prayers. Above all, let your love for one another be intense, because love covers a multitude of sins. Be hospitable to one another without complaining. As each one has received a gift, use it to serve one another as good stewards of God's varied grace." *(1 Pet 4:7-10)*

C. The Second Letter of Peter

1. Refuting false teachings based on apostolic authority

2. Awaiting the coming of the Lord

"But do not ignore this one fact, beloved, that with the Lord one day is like a thousand years and a thousand years like one day. The Lord does not delay his promise, as some regard 'delay,' but he is patient with you, not wishing that any should perish but that all should come to repentance. But the day of the Lord will come like a thief, and then the heavens will pass away with a mighty roar and the elements will be dissolved by fire, and the earth and everything done on it will be found out . . . . But according to his promise we await new heavens and a new earth in which righteousness dwells." *(2 Pet 3:8-10, 13)*

D. The Letter of Jude

"Jude, a slave of Jesus Christ and brother of James, to those who are called, beloved in God the Father and kept safe for Jesus Christ . . . ." *(Jude 1)*

1. Warning against false teachers

2. Prayer of praise

> "To the one who is able to keep you from stumbling and to present you unblemished and exultant, in the presence of his glory, to the only God, our savior, through Jesus Christ our Lord be glory, majesty, power, and authority from ages past, now, and for ages to come. Amen." *(Jude 24–25)*

LECTURE 8—THE BOOK OF REVELATION

I. Jesus Christ, the Alpha and the Omega, the beginning and the end

II. Apocalyptic literature

   A. Visions and symbols

   B. Not a forecast of the future—a "prophetic message"

   C. Crisis literature

   D. Victory over evil, sin, and death has been accomplished in Christ but is not yet fully realized

III. Content of the Book of Revelation

   A. John, exiled on Patmos

   B. Inaugural vision of Christ

      "When I caught sight of him, I fell down at his feet as though dead. He touched me with his right hand and said, 'Do not be afraid. I am the first and the last, the one who lives. Once I was dead, but now I am alive forever and ever. I hold the keys to death and the netherworld. Write down, therefore, what you have seen, and what is happening, and what will happen afterwards. This is the secret meaning of the seven stars you saw in my right hand, and of the seven gold lampstands: the seven stars are the angels of the seven churches, and the seven lampstands are the seven churches.'" *(Rev 1:17-20)*

C. Seven messages to the seven churches

D. Literary images with symbolic colors, numbers, animals, and places

"Then I saw standing in the midst of the throne and the four living creatures and the elders a Lamb that seemed to have been slain. He had seven horns and seven eyes; these are the [seven] spirits of God sent out into the whole world. He came and received the scroll from the right hand of the one who sat on the throne. When he took it, the four living creatures and the twenty-four elders fell down before the Lamb." *(Rev 5:6-8)*

E. Visions of seven seals, seven trumpets, and seven bowls

F. Climactic vision of the new creation—matrimonial union

"Then I saw a new heaven and a new earth. The former heaven and the former earth had passed away, and the sea was no more. I also saw the holy city, a new Jerusalem, coming down out of heaven from God, prepared as a bride adorned for her husband. I heard a loud voice from the throne saying, 'Behold, God's dwelling is with the human race. He will dwell with them and they will be his people and God himself will always be with them [as their God]. He will wipe every tear from their eyes, and there shall be no more death or mourning, wailing or pain, [for] the old order has passed away.'" *(Rev 21:1-4)*

IV. Symbols of the earthly liturgy reflect the eternal liturgy of heaven

V. The truth of Revelation endures in every age

    A. Hope in the future gives us strength in the present

    B. Living with the mystery of God's Word

QUESTIONS FOR STUDY AND DISCUSSION

1. St. Jerome said: "Ignorance of the Scriptures is ignorance of Christ."

   a. In what ways has reading and hearing the Scriptures helped you know Christ?

   b. How is St. Jerome's statement true of both the Old Testament and the New Testament?

2. The Old and New Testaments are the two parts of the one revelation of God through the Scriptures.

   a. What are the principal differences between the Old and New Testaments?

   b. In what way is the Old fulfilled in the New?

3. In the account of the Transfiguration (Matt 17:1-8), Jesus went up the mountain to pray. Here the glory of Christ is revealed to Peter, James, and John.

   a. What elements of this account indicate that Jesus completed the revelation given in the Old Testament?

   b. What did the appearance of Moses and Elijah add to the understanding of Jesus' identity?

4. Throughout history, many have sought to condense the four Gospels into one story of the life of Jesus.

   a. Why has the Church insisted on maintaining these four unique portraits of Jesus?

   b. What are some of the reasons the Gospels differ from one another?

5. Each Gospel is a two-level document—written from the historical context of both Jesus and the evangelist.

   a. How does the two-level nature of the Gospels make them different from pure biography?

   b. How does the context of your life today add another level of meaning to each Gospel?

6. Jesus' inaugural words and the heart of his message proclaimed: "The Kingdom of God/Heaven is at hand."

   a. Read God's promise to King David in 2 Samuel 7:16. How is God's promise fulfilled in the New Testament?

   b. Read the prophecy in Daniel 7:13-14. What do Jesus' references to himself as Son of Man in the Gospels tell you about the Kingdom (Matt 16:28)?

*Note: Some study questions deepen your understanding of what was learned in the previous lecture; other questions anticipate the material to be learned in the next lecture.

7. At times, Jesus seems to speak of the Kingdom of God/Heaven as already present; at other times, he speaks of it as not yet come.

   a. Determine which of the following passages from Matthew's Gospel speak of the Kingdom as a present reality and which speak of it as a future event: Matthew 5:3; 7:21; 12:28; 19:14; 25:34; 26:29.

   b. What do you think Jesus means by the "Kingdom of God/Heaven"?

8. Compare the Synoptic accounts of the Temptation of Jesus: Matthew 4:1-11; Mark 1:12-13; Luke 4:1-13.

   a. What elements are the same in every account?

   b. What are some of the main differences from one account to another?

9. Read the three parables of God's mercy in Luke 15.

   a. How do each of these parables express the concern of Jesus for those who are lost?

   b. Which of these parables touches your life most deeply? Why?

10. Compare the two forms of the Our Father given in Matthew (6:9-13) and in Luke (11:2-4).

   a. What are some of the differences you note?

   b. What could be some reasons for those differences? (Look at the context in each Gospel and the footnotes in your Bible for help.)

11. Compare the introductory verses of each of Luke's two volumes—
     Luke 1:1-4 and Acts 1:1-5.

     a. What does Luke indicate to be his purpose in writing?

     b. In what ways does Acts 1:1-5 link Luke's second volume with
         his first?

12. The last chapter of John's Gospel is often said to describe the role
     of the Risen Lord in his Church. Read John 21.

     What aspects of the Church do you think are represented by the
     miraculous catch, the lakeside meal, and the call of Peter? (The
     footnotes in your Bible may help.)

13. For a sample of Luke's descriptive writings, read Acts 27–28.

    a. Trace Paul's journey to Rome on a map as you read.

    b. Why is it appropriate that the narrative of Acts ends in Rome?

14. Compare Luke's description of Paul's call (Acts 9:1-9) with Paul's own account (Gal 1:11-17).

    a. What are the elements that these two accounts have in common?

    b. In what ways does Paul's experience compare to your own call in Christ?

15. Read each of the following passages in which Paul describes his evolving understanding of the Church: Acts 9:4; 1 Corinthians 12:27; Ephesians 1:22-23; and Colossians 1:24.

   a. How does Paul describe the relationship between Christ and the Church in each of these passages?

   b. How do these words of Paul challenge your understanding of the Church and your role within it?

16. In 2 Corinthians Paul's writing is remarkably autobiographical.

   a. List some of the physical hardships that Paul describes in 2 Corinthians 11:24-29.

   b. Read 2 Corinthians 12:7-10 for a description of Paul's afflictions. What do you think he means by the statement: "When I am weak, then I am strong"?

   c. In what ways have you seen the truth of Paul's statement in your own life?

17. Paul describes his pastoral ministry among the people in a variety of ways in his letters.

    a. Read 1 Thessalonians 2:7 and 2:11. What aspects of his ministry is Paul emphasizing here?

    b. Read 1 Corinthians 4:15 and Galatians 4:19. What do these images tell you about Paul's relationship to the people he served?

18. Though Paul was chained in prison, he expressed great joy as he wrote to the church in Philippi. Read Philippians 1.

    a. What are some of Paul's reasons for joy while in prison (Phil 1:3-7, 12-14, 18-21)?

    b. While in chains, Paul is caught between two desires (Phil 1:21-26). Why does his joy in Christ make both options desirable?

    c. In what ways do your experiences of Christian joy compare to Paul's?

19. Hebrews 11 reviews some of the people and events of the Old Testament as inspiring examples of faith.

   a. List the Old Testament names given in chapter 11, and list the book of the Bible in which their story is found.

   b. How would you describe the faith that unites their lives together?

20. The Letter of James emphasizes sound teaching and moral action. Read chapter 3 for some of his advice.

   a. What are the three images used by James to describe the power of speech (Jas 3:3-6)? What do all of these images have in common?

   b. What are some of the qualities of a wise person? Why is this type of wisdom so necessary for a Christian teacher?

21. The First Letter of Peter begins with an exhortation to the Church experiencing persecution. Read 1 Peter 1.

   a. Why does Peter describe the Christian experience of life as a "new birth" (vv. 3 and 23)?

   b. How does Peter encourage Christians to endure their trials?

   c. What advice in this chapter is most helpful for you?

22. The Book of Revelation frequently offers us a vision of the eternal liturgy in heaven which the Church's liturgy on earth reflects. Read Revelation 4.

   a. The "One seated on the throne" is the dominant image for God throughout the book. In what ways does this image energize and inspire your worship of God?

   b. The four angelic creatures symbolize all the creatures of the earth (Rev 4:6-8). What comparisons do you find between this image and those of the prophets in Isaiah 6:1-4 and Ezekiel 1:5-13?

23. The dominant image of Christ in the Book of Revelation is the Lamb. It is an image rooted in the Old Testament and expressed in several places in the New Testament.

   a. Read the following passages and comment on what they symbolically express about the historical deeds of Christ: Revelation 5:6; 7:14; 12:11; 19:7-9.

   b. Read the following passages from the Old Testament and describe the significance of the lamb (sheep) in each: Genesis 22:7-8; Exodus 12:5-7; Isaiah 53:7.

   c. In light of the Old Testament background, why does John's Gospel highlight Jesus as the Lamb of God (John 1:29)?

24. The final chapters of the Book of Revelation offer a symbolic vision of God's eternal Kingdom. Read Revelation 21–22.

   a. What symbols in this final vision demonstrate that God's Kingdom is a completion and perfection of the Old Testament?

   b. The Church is described in this vision as the bride of Christ. What comforts, hopes, and challenges does this image offer you?

NOTES